Vintage
French Interiors

Inspiration from the Antique Shops and Flea Markets of France

"Any object can become an *objet d'art* once put in a frame."

—*Boris Vian*

For Joseph and Lucien.
And for Laure, a perceptive advisor
and loyal accomplice on our adventures
in search of things vintage, without
whom this book would simply not exist.

Vintage French Interiors

Inspiration from the Antique Shops and Flea Markets of France

Text and photographs by Sébastien Siraudeau

Flammarion

Contents

Introduction

A twinkle of a crystal chandelier offset by a rough hewn farm table,

crisp embroidered linen pillow shams tucked next to a 1930s desk

clock—these are some of the exceptional details that can be culled

from *brocantes*—the flea markets and antique shops scattered

throughout France. The word *brocante* evokes a relaxed wander

in search for vaguely prescribed objects, useful or simply decorative.

Yet hunting for antiques and vintage items is also a passion. Fall for

a single thing and the appetite starts growing. A set of ninepins,

a Tonka truck, a Britannia tin box, a desk lamp, a milk jug,

a gilded mirror, a prettily worn door, or a wardrobe on its last

legs. Such a haul would easily fill the trunk of a Volvo station wagon.

But one doesn't need to be a "pro" to dig up something special.

Simply follow your nose and let yourself be carried away by the

unexpected beauty of the thing, by the story you imagine it might tell.

Let yourself be taken in by the brazen cheek of the dealer. Or else

satisfy that vital desire for something to embellish the house.

And, who knows, you might stumble across a bargain.

But where should you start looking? The following pages take you

on a journey through time and happenstance. From Paris to Brittany,

from Normandy to Provence, this book takes you on a flying visit to

France's best *brocantes*. More exactly, to the *brocanteurs'* stores.

The shopkeepers are all passionate about their business, all seek

to delight their customers, and endeavor to display their wares in

charming and surprising ways.

In some respects, and for some of these *brocanteurs*, this amounts

to a new profession: neither antique dealers nor interior decorators, but

people who unearth things—sometimes entire worlds.

What can one uncover in such shops? Seldom specialized, most

of the time the range of vintage goods available is wide and depends

on what has come in. Presented simply as they were found or given

a revamp, there may be religious trinkets, dishes, curios, signboards,

school desks, and nursery posters. There is paraphernalia from factories

or workshops, country crockery and kitchen utensils, dilapidated

shutters, items that whisk one back to the schoolroom. A plethora

of objects to decorate the home, to reuse, or just to recycle and save
from a pitiful and environmentally damaging end in the landfill.

Dare we mention money? Secondhand items are very often cheaper
than their new equivalent; you just have to appreciate the vagaries of
time. The recent fad for clearing out the attic and for garage and trunk
sales has certainly hiked up prices, for private buyers at least. What
is on sale in any given outlet depends not only on the store's location,
but also on where the object comes from: whether it has been dug out
from the back of a cupboard, bought from another dealer, purchased at
auction, or simply inherited. Once the dust settles, all should become
clear. Remember, you can stumble across a treasure at any time and in
any place. You just need sharp eyes and an insatiable curiosity. And in
the final analysis, a "fair" price is what you're prepared to fork over for
something you really want and which seems unique; it is the price you
pay for a feeling, for a pleasure. Because the *brocante* world is more than
a business, it's a way of life.

FLEA MARKET STYLE

The Saint-Ouen Flea Market

Montmartre

Batignolles

The Saint-Ouen Flea Market

MOMENTS & MATIÈRES

Puces de Saint-Ouen / Marché Vernaison
Allée 1, stands 13 and 27
93400 Saint-Ouen / 06 77 64 87 12
photos p. 12–19

The time when stall holders and ragmen used to set the Saint-Ouen flea market buzzing is long gone. This mecca of all things vintage, in which one can find absolutely everything, is now one of the most popular tourist venues in all of Paris; as many people are on the hunt for the odd and the rare as are taking a Sunday stroll. Among this tangle of markets, Marché Vernaison is the most intriguing. Winding one's way through its alleyways, the *Moments* stand comes as a surprise with its majestic and unique pieces,

such as a tailor's dummy
with a frozen smile, a gaping
bull's-eye or a sulky looking
papier-mâché rabbit, jostling
for position with scrap iron,
pieces of rotting wood, and
odd bits of armchairs. The
man who composed this
characterful little world,
Michel, says that he deals
in "the filth of the past," in
memories of private suffering
that make one want to touch,
to know more, to be moved.

CABINETS OF CURIOSITIES

Heavy if threadbare wall-hangings, broken industrial
furnishings, and giant shop signs—at first the stand of
Moments & Matières seems in step with the prevailing
zeitgeist, but one only has to pass over its inviting
threshold to find oneself plunged into a more original
and personal ambiance. Visitors are greeted by a plaster
bust of Napoleon III. Whetting the appetite, phonograph
horns converted into ceiling lights illuminate an anteroom
where yellowing volumes lie knowingly about. At the very
back of the stall, under the gentle glow from a chandelier
garlanded in jute, a skull (*vanitas, vanitatum!*) presides
over this wittily reconstituted *Wunderkammer* that harbors
some choice finds: shells, apothecary bottles, antlers,
bits of pilaster—all or any of which can, in a flash, whisk
one off on an improbable mental journey through time.

Montmartre

L'OBJET QUI PARLE...

86 rue des Martyrs / 75018 Paris

06 09 67 05 30

photos p. 20–23

I can safely say that my desire to write this book was kindled in the company of the friendly pair of eccentrics who run this place. *L'Objet qui parle…* sits between Pigalle and Abbesses, in the Paris of Amélie Poulain fame. A name, a shopfront, three walls, and that's it. Little more than a handkerchief—130 square feet perhaps—that Dominique and Guillaume reinvent every Monday when they return from their bargain hunting. Originally from Alsace, a region they often still scour, they always return with booty worthy of Ali Baba.

On a shelf cobbled together from wooden cotton reels—a neat bit of recuperation that was common enough in the textile-producing cities of Northern and Eastern France—is a motley stack of bowls, Viandox cups, old "Kub" stock-cube boxes, a wicker basket filled with etched glass test tubes.

All humor and tenderness, our two dealers compose these odds and ends into still lifes, making do with the blank stare of a puppet clown, a cuddly toy puppy, or one (of three) sardonic little piggies. As you excavate, your eye is drawn by kitsch ecclesiastical articles and other churchy knickknacks. Candlesticks, wedding bells, processional banners, nativity figures, and statues of angels rub shoulders with souvenirs from Lourdes and other holy curios—like the tiny brass hearts from the 1938 Marian Congress at Boulogne-sur-Mer, in which the pious would secrete their private hopes and prayers.

Just one of the lovely stories that *L'Objet qui parle...* is willing to share with us.

Batignolles

SOUS LES TOITS DE PARIS
1 place du docteur Félix Lobligeois
75017 Paris / 01 46 27 75 49
photos p. 24–29

Born in Paris but "made in Batignolles," (an area in north-west Paris), Gilles calls himself a "creator of environments." And ambiance is one thing *Sous les toits de Paris* enjoys in abundance. As soon as his first store opened up a stone's throw from the square des Batignolles, he'd sounded a revival in things vintage and started the *brocante* juices flowing. Every lightning visit turned into a conspiratorial discussion over a cup of tea. Times have changed and now Gilles has set up shop right on *the* place to be,

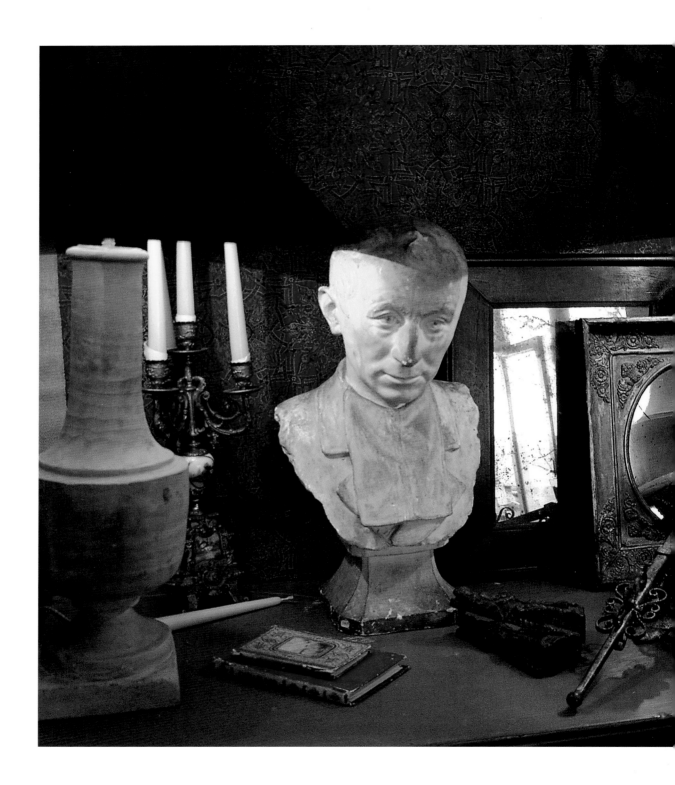

but he puts just as much energy into it as before.

A Nespresso machine may have replaced the old teapot, but the fun to be had in this ever-changing little theater remains constant, and the miscellany of objects in the teeming decor is still in a constant state of flux. Two lamps forged from pieces of a Charles X balcony and a pair of riding boots frame the stage. On a black-and-gold enameled tray, glazed plates rub shoulders with a couple of *boules* dressed in tartan. Here, a set of champagne flutes becomes a set of vases for the table; there, the juxtaposition of some specked mirrors and an austere looking stone bust offers food for thought.

Caring neither for style nor period, Gilles makes the most of his stock, be it rare or anecdotal, functional or functionless— to the point that today his services are sought as an interior decorator. Each new display affords its own batch of surprises and weirdness. New arrivals include a pair of polychrome columns from a seventeenth-century Provençal church that

frames a stack of chairs oddly held in place by hoops of rusty scrap metal.

Behind the door, one begins to understand the "cabinet of curiosities" urge that lies behind Gilles's creations. Dried butterflies, a bevy of stuffed deer, volumes with curling pages, all combine into a carefully contrived decor. Sometimes piled onto imposing pieces of furniture (an old counter, an architect's desk, a 1940s glass table), every display takes the form of a mini-museum dedicated to the object—novel, exquisite, intriguing—where a forlorn child's chair can tell the story of a life in the twinkling of an eye.

PARISIAN PANACHE

Rue Oberkampf
Near Popincourt
Marché Popincourt

Rue Oberkampf

ATELIER 154
Cité Durmar, 154 rue Oberkampf / 75011 Paris
06 62 32 79 06 /www.atelier154.com
photos p. 32–39

The cité Durmar is one of those retreats that bear witness to the enduring life of the Parisian outskirts. Artisans' workshops and artists' studios dot the verdant cobblestone cul-de-sac. At the very end, Stéphane Quatresous's studio is well attuned to the industrial heartbeat of the area. Wearing a trucker's jacket, a beanie pulled down low over his forehead, this *brocanteur* has, over time, begun to specialize in factory and workplace interiors, becoming a key resource for local architects and interior designers. Behind the misted glass frontage lurks a hodgepodge

of the kinds of industrial materials that have the less traditional decorators falling over each other. Whether it be a 1920s mail sorter or some Roneo filing cabinets or crates, Stéphane finds unexpected functions for pieces that prefigured so much of contemporary design, and he has no qualms about mixing them with a brace of Bertoia chairs or an Arne Jacobsen. Here, one can duly appreciate the ergonomics of a Bienaise Studio chair perched on its spidery legs or savor the modular chic of a piece by some anonymous handyman. But there's also the sculptural imagination of a tower of printer's blocks and the ballet-like elegance of a battalion of porcelain balloon molds, featuring coils, rabbits, ducks, and a collection of molded hands reaching skyward, freed from the famous kitchen gloves they used to sport!

WORK LAMPS

Not everyone has the means to acquire a heavy-duty workbench or a set of outsized shelves or tables. In the realm of industrial furniture, lighting is, from a practical point of view, far more accessible. First issued in the 1950s, the Jieldé standard lamp, with its articulated arm and its bulbous reflector equipped with circular handles—making it possible to adjust it without scalding one's fingers—is considered a classic. Rarer are lamps of the Gras style, with a cast-iron base or clamp, which illuminated the worktables of legendary architects such as Le Corbusier or Mallet-Stevens. The less ambitious will easily stumble across workshop or office lamps, telescopic bracket lights that look like insects, or the rows and rows of great enameled iron garage lights with which *Atelier 154* abounds.

Near Popincourt

LA MAISON
3 rue Neuve Popincourt
75011 Paris / 01 48 06 59 47
photos p. 40–41 and 43

ALASINGLINGLIN
14 rue Ternaux
75011 Paris / 01 43 38 45 54

TROLLS & PUCES
1 rue du Marché Popincourt
75011 Paris / 01 43 14 60 00
photos p. 4 and 42

BELLE LURETTE
5 rue du Marché Popincourt
75011 Paris / 01 43 38 67 39
photo p. 44–45

Blue-collar Popincourt. Paris *gouaille*—down-at-heel, rough-and-ready, but with a quick wit. Over the last few years, a whole brood of secondhand dealers has set up shop in spots all around the Marché Popincourt market hall. Nobody knows who arrived here first, but today the shopfronts are starting to form a none too orderly line-up worthy of the flea markets of yore. The visit kicks off at *La Maison*, which beckons us over with its bright turquoise frontage, "Pile-Poil" dog, and the enthusiasm of owner Eléonore, who has lost none of the verve she must have deployed when she worked in "communications." She is, then, an ideal ambassador for the band of artists, craftsmen, and former graphic designers who have been converted to selling antiques. And each does so in his or her own style: *Alasinglinglin* specializing in stuff from the 1960s to 1980s; *Trolls & Puces* is fond of trinkets and unlikely recyclings, like a screw-top canister from the legendary Weber Metaux, while its neighbor *Belle Lurette* is a jack-of-all-trades, selling everything from hollowware to industrial items.

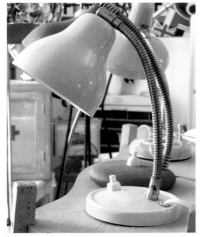

1950s–1970s BAZAAR

The 1950s, 1960s, 1970s—the early years of the whole "consumer society" shebang—can be found at Popincourt. And, in particularly good company at Eléonore and Dominique's *La Maison*, which gives a worthy foretaste of the Ikea generation. Articles both useful and decorative from the booming postwar years jostle for position: metal articulated desk lamps of every imaginable hue, design-style Formica clocks, generic ashtrays and glasses, a cardboard suitcase signed Vespa, an Air Inter cabin bag, an enameled Frigidaire advertising sign, a Polaroid camera.

This gives an idea of the kind of stuff they go in for around here, items snapped up by girls with manga haircuts in transit through Paris, neo-bohemians all misty-eyed about the the "old days" of merciless bartering, or freshly disembarked Parisians on the lookout for something to personalize their tiny apartment, something that'll raise a smile but won't break the bank.

Marché Popincourt

LA GARÇONNIÈRE
6 rue du Marché Popincourt / 75011 Paris
06 60 63 32 55 / www.lagarconniere.fr
photos p. 46–49

This is one of the newest *brocantes* in the district. With a wink to the bevies of girls who staff the nearby stores, "the boys" opened their *Garçonnière* in fall 2006 having cut their teeth elsewhere. (A *garçonnière* is a "bachelor pad"—and this one is a secret den especially for male lovers of vintage.) Though here and there one spots an errant doll or an old feather fan, the pickings in this tiny hideaway are for the most part "masculine." Not exclusively of course, but it has to be admitted that the backlit SENLIS-PARIS sign and the 1970s advertising bills for Michelin ZX tires would be more at home in an apartment belonging to someone with a taste for mechanical gizmos. Still, in *La Garçonnière* these objects have to compete for space with old mirrors, display units and bar tables, a postman's bicycle, and wooden lockers.

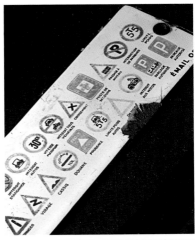

LETTERING, MARKERS, SIGNPOSTS

The *garçons* have a predilection for signposts and signs

in general, for the road or elsewhere, and have amassed

a collection of letters and numbers of every style: phone booth

signs, parking space numbers, old zinc lettering, an elevator

indicator, a board inscribed "Bois de Vincennes," a laminated

highway code crib sheet. The game consists in guessing the

period and then in discovering new uses or novel meanings:

rearrange the letters into someone's name or, failing this,

into your children's initials; invent weird and wonderful

acronyms; pick out your house number, your date of birth,

or an anniversary you should never forget. And all this fun

with letters and graphics is, of course, most edifying.

RIGHT BANK, LEFT BANK

The Marais
The Tuileries
Montparnasse

The Marais

AUX TROIS SINGES
23 rue Saint-Paul / 75004 Paris
01 42 72 73 69
photos pp. 52 to 57

AU BON USAGE
21 rue Saint-Paul / 75004 Paris
01 42 78 80 14

AU P'TIT BONHEUR LA CHANCE
13 rue Saint-Paul / 75004 Paris
01 42 74 36 38

LE COMPTOIR DU CHINEUR
49 rue Saint-Paul / 75004 Paris
01 42 72 47 39

Between the Seine and the Marais, the "village"

of Saint-Paul is a hallowed spot for antique hunting.

If dealers are losing ground to new design and art galleries,

a row of storefronts is putting up sterling resistance.

On one side there's a connoisseur of Thonet furniture

(*Au Bon usage*), on another there's a retro kitchen utensil

and stationary fanatic (*Au P'tit bonheur la chance*),

and a bells and whistles emporium (*Le Comptoir du chineur*).

Aux Trois Singes has set up residence right in the middle of this hodgepodge. Sylvain goes in for smarter wares, decorative for the most part. He sells, as he likes to put it, "useless" things. Just for the pleasure, the sheer futility of it. You just must have it, that thingamajig in the shape of a guy with a potbelly which is supposedly a German cigar cutter, or that candy box nestling in a papier-mâché Senegalese rifleman who looks as though he's stepped out of an ad for Banania chocolate drink. And there are larger items too, some on the monumental side, such as classic garden statuary and Medici vases in cast iron or stone. Enough to fill the park in one's country home—or else provide imaginative solutions for a balcony or a reception room back in town. After all, Sylvain (a landscape designer in a former life) specializes in what he loves most: garden furniture in the broadest sense.

THE ART OF THE GARDEN

Those traditional garden eye-catchers, Medici-style vases,

basins, and bowls regularly turn up at *Aux Trois singes*.

In addition to glass cloches and to eminently practical

metal watering cans, Sylvain has a fondness for anything

rocaille: pot stands, tables, and sculpture, such as the

papier-mâché mushrooms that reappear in the shopwindow

every fall. Chic at the beginning of the twentieth century,

these often unique pieces verge on folk art. Taking his cue

from the furniture on offer—cast-iron or scrap-metal tables

whose rough-and-ready patina (aka "grunge") he is careful

not to remove—Sylvain patiently tends these nature-inspired

trinkets, watering the moss that gathers on the hundred-year-

old cement every morning. For was it not Voltaire

who recommend we "cultivate our garden"?

The Tuileries

L'HEURE BLEUE
17 rue Saint-Roch / 75001 Paris
01 42 60 23 22
photos p. 58–61

Ah! That magic moment. Martine and Vincent have a thing about dusk, the gloaming—the "blue twilight hour." So in their little shop time is precious, so much so that they've installed their own lunar calendar. Every month and a half (on the dot), the decor gets a facelift. Come springtime it morphes into a Paris garden hideaway. Outside are earthenware jars, pots, shovels, pitchers, gardening books, dried flowers and growing racks, while behind the shutters an inviting landscape awakes beneath the starry glow

of a vast teardrop chandelier.
This lasts until the next
shake-up, which might see
a romantic castle appear,
or the cosy cocoon of one's
home after a long time away,
the heartwarming interior
of a chalet in Alsace, or,
in January—that traditional
month for all things white—
opulent heaps of bright
linen and jute.

Montparnasse

MAMIE-GÂTEAUX
70 rue du Cherche-Midi / 75006 Paris
01 45 44 36 63 / www.mamie-gateaux.com
photos p. 62–67

It's back to the pioneer days of the department store. We're on rue Cherche-Midi, a stone's throw from the famous Bon Marché emporium. Madame holds sway in the tearoom (hence, *Mamie-Gâteaux*) where light lunches pull in the crowds, while Monsieur orchestrates the adjacent *brocante* "corner shop" that refreshes its display each season. If the school term is under way, then rows of wooden or metal teachers' tables and pupils' desks spring up everywhere, as if this were a school museum. With a pencil case complete with inkstand, an exercise book

Plumier
le rossignol chante
le rossignol chante
le rossignol chante

inscribed with a hundred lines, a well-traveled geography textbook, a checkered apron or a graying smock, one is whisked back to the (good old) days of Mr. Chips. Luckily, the pigeonholes in a hardware storage cabinet are filled with plenty of fun things for recess: a jump rope or a bag of marbles filled with "shooters," "taws," "agates," and "steelies." Teatime beckons, so at the rear of the store Hervé Duplessis has rebuilt a postwar kitchen. From the venerable enameled iron stove to the nest of spice boxes, from the genteel chromolithograph to the dollhouse kitchen, everything here is carefully calculated to take one back to happier, simpler days.

SCHOOL POSTERS

Issued on a huge scale in the postwar period by the French
teachers' confederation—the Maison des Instituteurs—and
by publishers such as Rossignol and Bourrelier, schoolroom
posters sometimes make a welcome appearance at garage
sales in the country. At *Mamie-Gâteaux* they inevitably form
part of the decor, with some rarer specimens such as
botanical plates from the era of Napoleon III as well
as science, history, and language posters, or others
showing scenes from everyday life. Illustrated with talent
and individuality, by for instance, René Bresson and Hélène
Poirié, they often cast a candid light on the history
of an age that many remember with nostalgia. There are
the gardens (Luxembourg or the Tuileries?) with their endless
daily parades, or else the madcap adventures of Aline
and Rémi on the colored posters used for pronunciation
training, where it's all "*ba be bi bo bu.*"

FAMILY HEIRLOOMS

Neuilly

Boulogne

Neuilly

VERT DE GRIS
6 rue Ernest Deloison / 92200 Neuilly-sur-Seine
01 47 38 64 89

photos p. 70–73

She may have chosen "Verdigris" as her byline, but Élisabeth Brac de la Perrière has more than one pigment on her palette. Superficially austere with a color scheme dominated by the muted tones of beige, green, brown, and, inevitably, gray, this refined setting merely adds luster to her displays. For ten years now, people have been picking up Gustavian-style furniture here on a regular basis. Subtle patinas, sanded or scrubbed wood, rusted handles and fittings all speak volumes for Élisabeth's undeniable

talent; she is able to give zest to a chifforobe or a set of nineteenth-century chairs and dresser by adroitly adding that perfect and surprising accessory.

A natty footstool, some silver hotel tableware, a stack of medical textbooks from the 1800s, cast-iron plant pots, an architect's plan in faded ink, a basket filled with hooks and cream-colored shells, the bust—both grave and angelic— of a young Roman, a bizarre turquoise gable finial.

Élisabeth has a wonderful knack for that special finishing touch, for that affectionate detail, but also for concocting that alchemical moment when an old object meets its future purchaser. For, in the end, in life everything depends on meeting the right person.

Boulogne

AGAPÈ

91 avenue Jean Baptiste Clément
92100 Boulogne-Billancourt
01 47 12 04 88 / www.agapedeco.com
photos p. 74–81

Agapè literally means love. And *Agapè* does conjure up gloriously romantic images. Julie started out in the Scandinavian style of revival, cleaning, scraping, revamping doors and cupboards, tables and mirrors, dressers and chests of drawers.

An ideal homemaker-cum-Cinderella, this young *brocanteuse* has a taste for the tactile and she likes her furniture to flaunt its wear, to glow with a range of patinas from the lightest to the darkest shades. Gazing at a blackened desk scattered with curios,

one finds oneself imagining the torments of Baudelaire

completing *The Flowers of Evil*: "When the low and heavy

sky weighs down like a lid . . . "

And there is no shortage of lids since Julie has

a consuming passion for cutlery boxes and silver and ceramic

services, in particular for ivory faience soup tureens that

are always available, either in her shop here or at one of the

sales she organizes every year in a Paris apartment. For

three or four days, the space is bedecked with her most recent

discoveries and can be visited, and indeed used, like

a real house—from the office to the children's bedroom

(their portrait hangs on the wall), from the dining room

where the table stands ready and laid to the kitchen where tea

is on hand accompanied by some *biscuits roses* from Reims.

BOXES

Lids, once again. Lids for containers of every kind that one accumulates and piles into heaps over generations, hoping they might one day come in useful. Here there are gems ready to be discovered by the curious: sweet canisters, paint boxes, musical boxes, first aid kits, letter boxes, card index boxes, cookie tins, shoe boxes, toolboxes, hatboxes. *Agapè* is clearly afflicted with this obsessive madness—or aggravating phobia—proposing an original composition made up of tricolor Bolduc ribbon boxes or English bread tins, or else pyramids of cotton reel boxes picked up in a textile factory in northern France, which could be recycled as perfect bottomless toy boxes. A real box of treats!

RARE FINDS

Picardy
The Picardy Coast
Lille

Picardy

LA BROCANTE DE LA BRUYÈRE
32 rue Campion / 60880 Le Meux
03 44 91 12 77
photos p. 84–87

Picardy—from Survilliers to Amiens via Crèvecoeur-le-Grand
or Abbeville—is no stranger to junk markets and *réderies*, as they
call garage sales here. *La Brocante de la Bruyère* is planted
in one of those red-brick farms so characteristic of the region's
countryside. Although not far from the well-heeled cities
of Chantilly and Senlis, one can still come across some great
"steals" that make out-of-town *brocantes* so much fun. With
a hearty nod in the direction of the famous racecourse nearby,

our eye was initially caught by a stable of model horses. Then, all higgledy-piggledy, one comes across an embroidered alphabet primer, a rusty Tolix-type stool, wooden toys, zinc vanes, and a weathercock. And this is just a tiny sample of the unfussy stock Florence has arranged in her gorgeous country farmstead.

The Picardy Coast

BORDS D'EAUX
35 rue Jules Barni / 80350 Mers-les-Bains
02 35 50 12 65
photos p. 88–91

PATRICK DELOISON
1 quai Romerel / 80230 Saint-Valéry-sur-Somme
03 22 26 92 17

What people adore about Mers-les-Bains are the madcap rococo villas from the I-do-like-to-be-at-the-seaside years, as well as the cheerfulness of its garage sales, all of which augures well for picking over the *brocantes*, from the Alabaster Coast to the bay of the Somme. One might net a batch of wooden decoy ducks at Patrick Deloison's in Saint-Valéry, or a mechanical toy such as a "jumping rabbit" or a "pecking chicken"—refugees from the 1980s—at *Bords d'eaux*. Geoffroy Dassé inherited these entertaining items from his

mom, who used to run a novelty beach store. He has lost
nothing of his childhood's adventurous imagination, which
he exercises daily in his business activities. And he has
a whale of a time, too, jumbling up periods, making
the sparks fly, and all because he loves working outside
the square, because he chose his profession for the fun,
and he never wants it to become a chore. Today, it's a
vintage rocking chair signed Charles Eames that lords it
in the middle of the shop, fraternizing with an eighteenth-
century table, Napoleon III and "Tulip" chairs, and a slew
of decorative articles ranging from the 1950s to the present
day, such as a silicone vase by Italian designer Gaetano
Pesce. There's no telling what tomorrow will bring. Though
one thing you can bet on is that by then Geoffroy will have
repainted the walls and shopfront of his "games room".

Lille

The first Sunday in September, Lille unpacks its treasures at a gargantuan annual sale that pulls in amateurs and dealers alike, a bantering *brocante* that features everything from cake molds upwards. Aside from this unmissable ritual, vintage-lovers might also venture into the byways of a more mysterious Lille. Under the glass roof in *Espace Nord-Ouest* at Bondues, the dealers' stands almost look like Captain Nemo's cave, where a trio of carnival "grotesques" is not half as scary as the collection of bottles

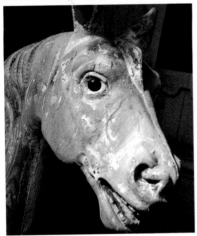

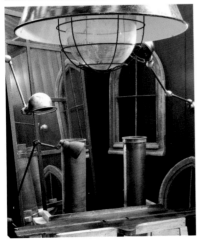

of reptilian creatures pickled in formaldehyde. There
are no half measures here: "We go for the grandiose."
A huge stretch of wainscoting, a bearskin employed as a door
hanging, gigantic metal pigeonhole units studded with rivets,
a larger-than-life wooden horse, and two stone eagles ready
to swoop on their prey. More sensitive souls should make
for the welcoming haunt at Marcq-en-Baroeul *Brokidée*.
Every room in this onetime Flemish farm offers choice
pickings, from the kitchen to the boys' bedroom via an airing
cupboard teeming with trousseaus for the debutante daughters
of the great families of the North. Finish up with a spot
of tea or a tasty tart in the hushed decor of the tearoom-cum-
vintage store at *Tous les jours Dimanche*… in the heart
of Lille's old town.

GAMES AND TOYS

If one wasn't born with the heart and soul of a collector,

chasing down old games and toys can still be a real pleasure,

not only because they are such obvious fun, but also because

inexorably they take you back to your childhood. And some

of these toys—whether they be ones we once lost and have

forgotten or never even knew existed—are priceless treasures.

A pedal car or a rusty tricycle, a clutch of stripy skittles, the

frog game (you can still find them in the north of France),

a lawn croquet set, a bulk load of Majorettes, some vintage

Playmobils, are all more than enough incentive to open

one's wallet. And so it is with this Meccano set spotted at

Le Marchand d'Oublis (right next to *Espace Nord-Ouest*)

with which one already imagines building an insane mechanical

apparatus, some quirky Eiffel Tower or an ocean-going

contraption fitted out to dive 20,000 leagues under the sea!

CLASSIC DISTINCTION

From Rouen to Trouville
Near Cormeilles

From Rouen to Trouville

FANNETTE W.
93 rue d'Amiens / 76000 Rouen
02 35 73 49 77
photos p. 100–103

LA VIE À LA CAMPAGNE
39 rue Haute / 14600 Honfleur
02 31 88 47 83

MISE EN SCÈNE
76 rue des Bains / 14360 Trouville-sur-Mer
02 31 81 91 55
photos p. 104–105

From the banks of the Seine to the coast, Normandy's long and winding roads are flanked by countless *brocantes*. One just has to stop at Rouen, between the famous town clock and its vertiginous cathedral. Here, Fanette W., daughter of an antique dealer from Lyon, energetically pilots a going concern in curios, tradesmen's tools, and smaller pieces of country furniture, located behind the traditional half-timbered houses of the rue Eau-de-Robec. The eye first alights on a strange totem studded with nails, a big plaster

nose, a birdcage, a draper's rule, a worn chest of drawers, before flitting on to some wooden statuettes. The collection of diverse portraits—hung as if in some humanist's private gallery—gets Fanette talking, and the unknown sitters gradually come into focus, such as "her" gypsy or "her" little gent, who, in spite of their reticent looks, turn heads. Among all the canvases, there are naturally some seascapes painted in oils, in which schooners and three-masters tell the story of the harbor of a hundred bell towers.

From the quayside, the Seine winds down to Honfleur and the seaside resorts of the now flourishing coast, where—from the enchanting *La Vie à la Campagne*, dedicated to every conceivable type of garden article, to the well-named boutique of *Mise en Scène* at Trouville— vintage and antique dealers are part of the landscape.

Near Cormeilles

LA SERRE
Route de Cormeilles / 14130 Bonneville-la-Louvet
02 31 64 03 21
photos p. 106–111

In the Auge region, a few miles from the sea, we come across this spectacular "greenhouse." Cleared of the waste and of the ivy in which it was once shrouded, it now shelters a curious kitchen garden. Four top-drawer *brocanteurs* concoct strange "pick-and-mixes" that wed the rare with the outlandish: one of them, leader of the gang and head of the academy, is clearly up to speed on twentieth-century interiors, with a collection of riser chairs and comfy leather numbers. Another one strips factories and robs

banks—but just for their
unique furnishings: hefty
filing cabinets, steel
pilasters, imposing light
fittings, substantial—but
empty—Fichet safes.
A third has unearthed
counters and other
oversized pieces of
workshop paraphernalia,
while the last adds
a romantic touch with a
selection of painted wood
furniture and venerable
chests of drawers.

ART AND TECHNOLOGY

That old dichotomy of art and technology doesn't only provide

philosophers with food for thought: it also has pride of

place beneath *La Serre*'s glass roof. Craftsmen's equipment,

scientific apparatus, elaborate mechanisms of all sorts are

liberated from their erstwhile function and exhibited as works

of art. Though unsigned, an array of iron sorting tables from

the Banque de France seem to bear the stamp of Gustave

Eiffel. Meanwhile, a hand-printing press, some lightbulbs,

batteries, and a set of factory clocks under glass take flight

as ornamental sculptures. An architect's desk complete

with rulers, set-squares, and protractors, an optician's

apparatus or a copper surveyor's range finder, a Napoleon III

cast-iron photographer's stand, or just plans and diagrams

for mechanical tools all lead us, of course, into the world

of the engineer—but also into the world of the inventor,

that artist of the useful and the necessary.

NATURAL BEAUTY

Rémalard

La Perrière

Bellême

Nogent-le-Rotrou

Rémalard

LA MAISON FASSIER
55 rue de l'Eglise / 61110 Rémalard
02 33 73 56 21
photos p. 114–121

A host of angels. The Fassiers have been cultivating the art of *brocante* for thirty years and their store in the Perche is all about art: an art that borders on the mysterious and the mystical. Still, there's nothing more down-to-earth than the collections they tirelessly amass and offload: sturdy pieces of trade furniture, broad-shouldered workbenches, gears and springs, stuffed animals, and many unlikely curios. But the way their store is arranged transports us to the world of an imaginery science museum, covering everything from the Enlightenment to the industrial era. This off-kilter universe has recently settled into a fitting space—that is, in a grand former girls' boarding school right in the center of Rémalard called, aptly enough, "Ange Gardien" (guardian angel). A moss-covered celestial guardian still watches over the park to the rear of the imposing heap that remarkably, has been converted into a grand house by the couple, who give their "homemaking" talents full rein here. On the ground floor

a long corridor embraces kitchen, linen room, workshop, and
cabinet of curiosities. Each room fulfills its role, and life
transpires in incredible still lifes and compositions. One is
already struck by the carefully stage-managed lighting
of the kitchen, accentuated by taxidermed birds, such as
the ducks strung up as if after a morning shoot and the hens
one can almost still hear cackling. The effect is further
strengthened by the sense of touch—by the muscular materials,
the rough-and-ready boards, the oily metals and glowing copper,
the fragments of stone columns and pediments, the dog-eared
books and papers tied up with string, and, finally, the old
fabrics and cloths from linen to flax, all given new life
by Claudia Fassier. The curios and the workshop are
Alain's domain; where he displays a collection of wood and
bark in abstract shapes that gives one a sense of the artistic
heart of *La Maison.*

ANIMALS

Together with herbals, seashells, and stones, animals are

an essential ingredient in any cabinet of curiosities worthy of

its name. Alain Fassier has a special liking for birds,

from peacocks to geese; some are shown under glass, others

are in the open, hailing visitors to his *Maison*. As such pieces

tend to be associated with hunting and its trophies, they do not

always find favor, in spite of their disconcertingly expressive

beauty. Nonetheless, a number of them are the fruit of the

progress made by taxidermy in the eighteenth and nineteenth

centuries, when the aim was to satisfy the thirst for knowledge

in natural history among both gentlemen scholars and lovers

of the weird and wonderful. Rather than the crocodiles

or vanished reptiles, one might prefer a wooden anatomy model,

a little carving of a lamb, a stone deer, or butterflies

and beetles mounted under glass, which would delight any child

who has dreamed of making Noah's Ark as much as it

would an entomologist.

La Perrière

LA MAISON D'HORBÉ
Le Bourg / 61360 La Perrière
02 33 73 18 41
photos p. 122–125

Still more angels. While hiking through the groves and valleys of the Perche it's impossible not to stop at *La Maison d'Horbé*, located on the main square of the town of La Perrière. Since lingerie icon Chantal Thomass extolled its wonders on French television the store has become a sensation. Its story stretches back long before that, however, some fifteen years to be precise, when Jean-Noël and Julien deserted Paris and first took on the seventeenth-century ruin which they have now converted to

a country *brocante*.Concerned by the preservation of
the region's heritage, they have renovated the place bit by bit,
investing themselves in the history of the village. Julien writes.
Jean-Noël hunts for jewelry from Asia or porcelain from China
and elsewhere, for silver canteens, secret boxes, chemists'
phials, and for all kinds of curios that make digging through
the bric-a-brac here such a delight. In 2002, the duo was
joined by Laurent and *La Maison d'Horbé* opened
a tearoom serving a light but luxury menu including foie gras
or scallops, depending on the time of year. The *Maison*
has since developed into a meeting place where one can
run into all sorts of people—tourists, locals, and any of
the countless Parisians who have made this neck of the
woods their home. One chats about life, swaps stories,
and then makes off with something to decorate the house—
because even if life's other joys can be ephemeral, this isn't!

Bellême

GABRIELLE FEUILLARD
10 rue Ville-close / 61130 Bellême
02 33 73 53 82
photos p. 126–127

A newcomer to the lanes of Bellême, the boutique *Gabrielle Feuillard* fits in comfortably with the other landmarks of its genre in the region. It is run by Antony Adam, who is at once the local florist and a dealer in vintage interiors.

Renewed every season, the decor—tended as lovingly as any greenhouse—toys with every style, from baroque to fin de siècle. The diminutive space, structured by a lawyer's filing cabinet or an old shop counter, is then filled with a miscellany of interesting finds: weighty tomes on which time has left its mark, a clutter of candelabras, statues of the Virgin, stoups, crosses, antique frames, even a terra-cotta bust of Molière. Flowers, from old roses to chrysanthemums, naturally grace the backdrop created by this onetime fine art student, who takes his inspiration from the rhythms of the countryside—something his grandmother, the eponymous Gabrielle, taught him.

Nogent-le-Rotrou

VILLAGE DU VAL D'HUISNE

RN23 direction Nogent-le-Rotrou

28400 Nogent-le-Rotrou

06 86 93 10 15

photos p. 128–133

As one might expect, France's major roads are peppered with countless *brocantes* and *dépots-vente*, or consignment shops. Loudly proclaimed by signs and piles of hoardings, they form a disorderly queue along many routes popular among *brocante* dilettantes on their travels.

The national highway just outside Nogent-le-Rotrou is no exception to the rule. Taking over the site of a former service station, four *brocanteurs* have joined forces in a village in

the Valley of the
Huisne. Having cut
their teeth in the
Parisian markets of
Vanves and Saint-Ouen,
these four battle-worn
musketeers now ply
their trade in this
pleasant bit of country
in the Perche. All four
have created their own
little worlds in their
shops in the "village":
there's Marie, who
goes in for curios,
sophisticated vintage,
and scullery and pantry

furniture; and Philou, who has a remarkable nose for religious trinkets—from large-scale depictions of the stations of the cross down to humble crucifixes—though there are pagan gewgaws too, including a mighty collection of 1970s plastic costume jewelry. . . . Rather than Merchants in the Temple, then, this happy lot of eclectic dealers together offer bargain-hunters scouring the national highways a chance to make some unexpected discoveries—and indulge in a spot of time travel. If you're lucky, you might stumble across a wooden propeller from who-knows-what lunatic UFO, a set of Napoleon III globes, or an unbreakable wooden "Dejou" children's truck, which long ago you may have pedalled around the living room yourself—you never know.

After all, the most rewarding journey any vintage-lover can make is the one that goes back in time, to childhood.

A TOUCH
OF ROMANCE

On the Banks of the Loire
Dahouët
Plélo

On the Banks of the Loire

  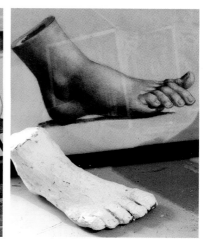

ANGES ET DÉMONS
14 rue Notre Dame / 49350 Cunault
06 03 56 09 26
photos p. 136–141

Every angel has a demon. On the banks of the Loire, between the ancient hamlets, the manor houses, and the four-star châteaux, the village of Cunault is noted above all for its Romanesque church. And it is at the foot of this masterpiece that Sophie Prételat has elected to dwell. She's been into antiques since she was ten and remembers cycling about here as a child netting butterflies. She preserves the passion for freedom that led her to become a *brocanteuse* intact. Often out and about, inquisitive about

everything, her little ark is packed with a wealth of vintage fare. Every piece of her collection brings a new surprise, with a jumble of unsophisticated and more elevated wares, laid out in lively compositions that invade every nook and cranny of the house. If a puppet that has seen better days shares a shelf with a colorful Santibelli Virgin, a nameless nude with a collection of boxes and wooden flask cases, every one of these objects has a story that Sophie tells with enthusiasm. Often wide-eyed with wonder, as today before a batch of large engravings by Jean-Baptiste Oudry illustrating La Fontaine's *Fables*, she is never above confessing ignorance, reminding us that there is always much to learn, so much so that the demons of this enigmatic and delectable purgatory never fail to lead us into temptation.

Dahouët

The facade is red—as red as the old cigarette packs with the picture of Uncle Sam that Roland has a fetish for collecting. This "end of the world" is, however, neither in America nor on some treasure island, but in a hangar in a small Breton port. Gleaned from flea markets, Roland's multifarious vintage discoveries range from fine antiquities to more bizarre objects: there are paintings by minor Breton masters as well as old toys and tin soldiers, while an Isle-Adam terra-cotta graces the window display. An evocative collection of *Fisherman Return*s and other picturesque scenes and figures smacks of seaside holidays at Dahouët—or wherever you spent yours.

AU BOUT DU MONDE
Quai des Terre-Neuvas / 22370 Pléneuf-Val-André
02 96 63 18 84
photos p. 142–143

Plélo

**LA MAISON BLEUE
(AT THE CHAR À BANC)**

Moulin de la Ville Geffroy / 22170 Plélo

02 96 74 13 63

photos p. 144–149

In Brittany, the *Char à Banc* is a name known to all. This farm and adjacent mill was converted into an all-purpose inn in the 1970s and here the Lamour family busies itself serving unpretentious fare, airing guestrooms, and amusing children. Their taste for old things and their love of local heritage snowballed, and the premises have even housed an agricultural eco-museum with an old plow and tractors on their last wheels. *La Maison Bleue*, nestled in the basement of the

four-hundred-year-old granite mill, was the brainchild of
Jeanne, the mom and now grandmother of this hardworking
troop. A tireless hunter of vintage pieces, you don't need
to be told that Jeanne has an insatiable appetite for old
crockery. The *brocante* overflows with cabinets full of
faience and tin utensils, but also with more rustic objects,
from zinc pitchers to a cute statuette of the Virgin which
in former times would have watched over hearth and home.
Still, it would all be far less effective without the displays
in red, green, blue, and yellow composed by one of her
daughters, Céline, into a homey environment that encourages
enthusiastic excavation.

GRANDMA'S KITCHEN

Piles of plates and terrines, towers of ramekins and cups,

batches of glasses, dishcloths and tea towels, enameled

kettles and coffee jugs, drainers and strainers, soup tureens,

casseroles, and saucepans. *La Maison Bleue* deals in the

most delightful kitchenware. In this well-lit and (deliberately)

chaotic bazaar, once common objects begin to acquire

the allure of a unique piece. Even if you come across the

odd crack, chip, or nick, it hardly matters as there are enough

dishes here to compose a week's worth of table settings

and services. From pieces from the Digoin et Sarreguemines

workshop—with its floral or geometrical patterns that go so

well with the subtle blue of a Saint-Uze piece—to the cream-

colored Gien collection, or a cracked Charolles dish, the stock

offers a tour of French crockery. And don't forget to grab a jar

of *Char à Bancs*'s homemade rhubarb jam on your way out.

RUSTIC CHARM

Bordeaux
Cap-Ferret
Île de Ré

Bordeaux

PASSAGE SAINT-MICHEL

Passage and Hangar Saint-Michel

14, 17 place Canteloup / 33800 Bordeaux

05 56 92 14 76 / www.passage-st-michel.com

photos p. 152–159

Bordeaux. The elegant capital of the southwest is experiencing a shake-up, with the quaysides undergoing a facelift, and whole districts being pedestrianized: it's now a place to saunter. Close to the Garonne river, the place Saint-Michel has lost nothing of its soul though. Cosmopolitan and spawned from a tradition of craft and commerce, the market attracks the usual dose of antique hunters, strollers, and junk dealers. In front of the flea market, the Passage Saint-Michel offers a mixed bunch of stands over several stories.

Laurence's stand at the entrance—with tons of sculpture ranging

from the monumental to the minuscule (like this battalion

of Orientalist miniatures)—gives a taste of the time travel to

come. Is it bric-a-brac, or a real antique? It's hard to tell as, eyes

peeled, one crisscrosses this vintage "department store"—it now

extends into a hangar once belonging to the Giffrer firm—that

has been revamped by three retro addicts. Among the apparent

pandemonium, the personality of each comes through: there's

Ludovic, a former graphic designer, who presents a highly

idiosyncratic cabinet of curiosities; Laurent, whose explosive

decors can also be experienced at his gallery on the Île de Ré;

and Jamel, who schleps his stock of industrial wares to

the Quinconces fair, the huge biannual junket for *brocanteurs*

from the southwest.

TOOLS AND MATERIALS

Rarely escaping the wrath of demolition contractors,

old building materials are becoming increasingly rare.

For every ceramic basin or batch of cement tiles saved,

how many cast-iron baths are shattered by a sledgehammer?

How many iron railings and walls have been flattened

by a bulldozer? It's a cruel, cruel world. And, for strippers

and secondhand dealers alike, building materials are as

troublesome as they are hard to take down, transport,

and revamp. So, turning regretfully away from a pair

of oaken doors, a garden statue, or an entire stone mantelpiece,

one settles for less weighty wonders, such as an ornamental

pelmet (a single piece of which would be enough to decorate

a wall in a reception room) or these masonry trowels

still caked in dried plaster that might make an original

corner shelf, or a set of resin pots that would impart a modestly

elegant touch to any balcony.

Cap-Ferret

L'ESPRIT DU CAP

2 rue des Pionniers / 33950 Lège-Cap-Ferret

05 56 60 67 79

photos p. 160–163

Now we've reached the ocean and the Bassin d'Arcachon that nestles between the dunes of Pilat and Cap-Ferret and where Stéphane Bugot has established, right at the end of the spit, his most recent pied-à-terre. A descendant from a line of three generations of antique dealers, Bugot spent time at the Louvre (where the antique stores are) and then opened his first boutique at Saint-Cloud on the outskirts of Paris, before escaping into a career in luxury goods. His notion of luxury has changed now too: the sea, a good book, a good

sweater, and a good armchair. Hence *L'Esprit du Cap*, where even the sign comes as a surprise: ANTIQUITÉS – SPORTSWEAR. There are sweaters obviously, but the label reads "handwoven" and they are accompanied by a splendid panorama of coastal vintage wares. Paneled in faded blue-painted pine, the "Spirit of the Cape" satisfies every desire for the ocean—whether you're an old sea dog or a landlubber. From yacht furniture to long-haul trunks, from solid captain's chairs to lanterns and other maritime necessities, in burnished copper and dark wood, naturally; there's a folding-screen, a 1900s cane deckchair, a wardrobe in pitch pine, a bamboo console table for the stay-at-homes, and, on the walls—a further invitation to distant climes—a collection of pictures and marines, of which at least one will feature an ancient transatlantic steamship.

And, as a fitting end, there's the inevitable inkstand made of painted shells, mussels, scallops, and mother-of-pearl that betrays the nostalgic heart of the place.

Île de Ré

LA TREILLE MARINE
4 place de la République / 17410 Saint-Martin-de-Ré
05 46 09 36 22
photos p. 164–169

On this island devoted to all things decorative, antique hunting has become a way of life and each village on Île de Ré has plenty to choose from. There's the *Bigorneau Langoureux* at La Flotte, *Campani* at Saint-Martin, *Galerie Kahn*, *Côté Jardin*, *Boutique*, and *20*—where one can grab a drink as well—at Ars. Off the beaten path, however, one comes across *La Treille Marine*. Danielle pays no heed to the weather or time of the day, and throws back her shutters whenever she fancies. So, *La Treille* has no opening hours as such, and you just have to be

lucky to enter this bohemian
(not to say eccentric) little
world. A born storyteller,
our *brocanteuse* creates
touching scenarios in which
every element is selected and
positioned with immense care.
Everything has a role: for
Easter weekend, for instance,
Danielle arranges a meeting
between a scuffed Christ,
a chocolate rabbit, and a bird
and some eggs fallen from
a nest. When the moment
comes to open up shop,
however, the storybook is
closed again, because Danielle

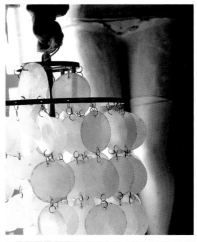

reuses each figure in another decoration, so that its tale
vanishes without trace. The only evidence left of the "bride's
story" she concocted out of a disembodied pair of wooden
legs and a bit of taffeta, adorned with some rice grains
and a few pearly pendants, is a fleeting memory recorded in
a misty photograph. One can imagine a whole life unfolding
in a composition made up of a photograph of a communicant,
some medallions, a rosary, a music score, and a crucifix,
all pinned to a partition constructed of scraped-down
floorboards. After briefly communing with nature in her
secret garden—an authentic Île de Ré plot filled, as one might
expect, with evocative set pieces—Danielle sets out once
again into the countryside to track down materials for a new
page in her very personal Book of Hours.

BURIED TREASURE

Near Lyon

Isle-sur-la-Sorgue

Banon

Near Lyon

LES PUCES DU CANAL

1 rue du Canal / 69100 Villeurbanne
04 72 04 65 65 / www.pucesducanal.com
photos p. 172–179

It's Sunday morning and Lyon has hardly stirred. But at the flea market *Les Puces du Canal*, the day is already well under way, as anyone with a passion for antiques will have invaded the well-stocked hangars at dawn. Over the years, the *brocanteurs* have gradually deserted the fancier locations in the city for this weekly get-together at the *puces* market. One's eye is immediately caught by Aisle G and the industrial furnishings and outsized alphabet on Didier's stand. A flea's jump away is Aisle F—that's

F for Florence, who shows a flair for trade and industrial furniture, which she combines with creations made of old burlap cushions or mattresses. The same clever knack is to be found at Louise's stand a few feet away, and also on Cécile's stand, *Patines* that stocks some wonderful and very collectible trade and shop signs (CHARCUTERIE, or butcher; a red TABAC sign in the shape of a carrot).

TRADE AND WORKSHOP FURNITURE

Made-to-measure, unique, reeking with nostalgia for the skills of yesteryear—today, anything with a link to bygone trades and crafts is much sought after. A draper's worktop, a seed rack, a board for clocking-in cards, a set of workshop lockers, and a hardware storage unit still with its stenciled numbers—and the decor is in place. Florence might briefly return a set of wooden shoehorns, some reels of copper wire, some tinplate cookie molds, flasks, and glass bottles, or some mother-of-pearl buttons, to their original use before morphing them into a reception room console table, a rotating photo stand, a business card container, a bookshelf, or even a wardrobe for a child's bedroom. With a glass of white wine in hand, one mulls over one's latest purchases and tries to work out how to get all the stuff home!

Isle-sur-la-Sorgue

  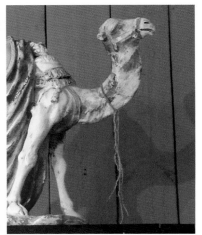

LA CARAVANE PASSE
Christine and Denis Nossereau
7 avenue des 4 Otages / 84800 L'Isle-sur-la-Sorgue
04 90 38 25 86
photos p. 180–187

CAFÉ-DÉCO
1 avenue des 4 Otages / 84800 L'Isle-sur-la-Sorgue
04 90 38 38 16

LA PETITE CURIEUSE
23 rue de la République / 84800 L'Isle-sur-la-Sorgue
04 90 20 86 59

L'Isle-sur-la-Sorgue. This dazzling little town in eastern Provence with its daily markets is an essential stopover on any vintage binge. From hangars to storerooms, from *Café-Déco* to *La Petite curieuse*, it's a game of leapfrog crossing all the bridges over the Sorgue. At the start of the trail comes the Île aux Brocantes, an urban island and a real treasure trove, while the waltz ends beneath the vine trellis in the Nossereaus' new outlet which, without quite knowing why, Christine christened *La Caravane*

passe. It was in all probability because theirs is no fledgling talent, but has been maturing since their earlier forays in the nearby little town of Manosque. With barely a glance at the fashions that come and go, they follow their (own) noses and, with a nicely personal touch, it is their stories, their travels, their encounters that feed into this little oasis, filling it with wooden horses, leaky stuffed bears, cement birds, and other beasts. A crack, a mere scratch, and one is promptly plunged into some distant memory, real or imaginary.

POPULAR ART

The caravan passes, the dogs bark, but popular art goes

on forever. Far from art school, these long-abandoned

or long-forgotten objects were handcrafted by anonymous

or marginal artists, and they often betray genuine skill.

Carved miniatures or toys, stone statuettes, scraps of

wood and iron, nailed, glued, welded into shape, these

untutored creations—utilitarian or useless—come in all

shapes and sizes. Without parallel, this world is the soul

of *brocante*. It finds a perfect haven with Christine

and Denis Nossereau, whose arrangements are works

of art in their own right rather than mere displays.

The value of their discoveries lies in their scarcity, in

a tremulous beauty each customer perceives through the lens

of his or her individual sensibility and sincerity. And in the

final analysis, it is this that bestows on them such vibrancy.

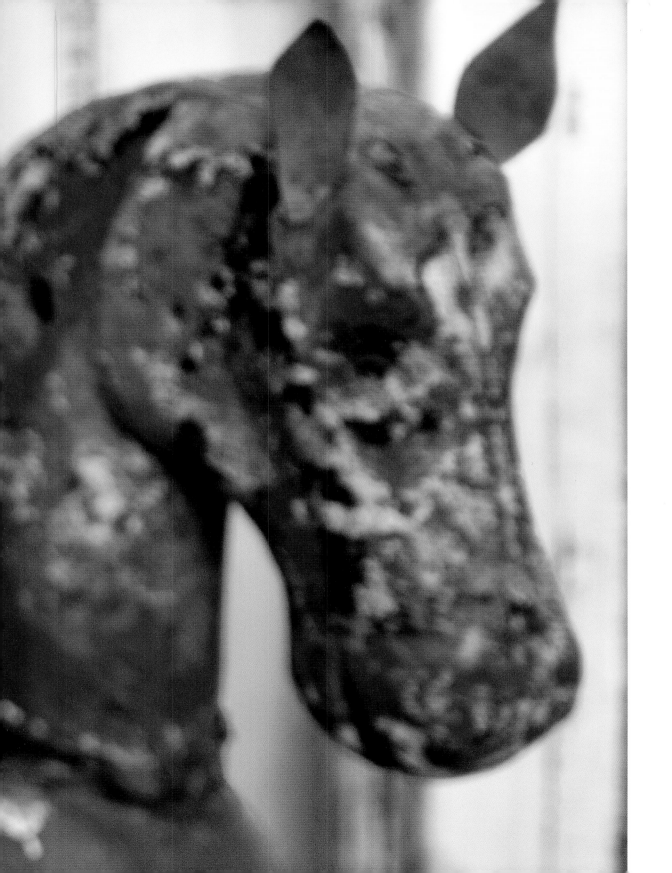

Banon

LES BONS MOMENTS

Place Saint-Just / 04150 Banon

04 92 73 39 94

photos p. 188–193

For this journey's end, just follow the signposts to Banon,

a village in Haute-Provence, with its delicious eponymous cheese,

glorious bookshop, and, not far off, a *brocante*/tearoom aptly

dubbed *Les Bons Moments*. Ideal for whiling away the "good

times" at Banon—such is the philosophy of Marie and Péroline

who run this cheerful, laidback venue. As a reward for coming

so far, they greet you as if in a road house—but one where tarts

and teas from the world over are served to warm the heart, and

BROCANTE
SALON de THE
BROCANTE
SALON de THE
sur jardin
"Les bons moments"
GALERIE

which contains a gallery proposing writing workshops and
temporary exhibits. As if to repudiate the rarely acknowledged
loneliness of a trade they used to practice alone, our two
accomplices encourage conversation and introduce people
against the constantly changing, indeed "takeaway" backdrop
that is their store. One used to specialize in period linen,
the other in silverware—and now variety is their specialty.
A Louis XV *bergère* chair, some dentist's furniture, a little
Chinese chest of drawers, a picture showing the parched
mountains of their region—they have no preconceived style,
because what they revel in most is diversity and storytelling,
ideas they sum up in two words: "absolute bliss!"

CHAIRS

No games of musical chairs here, for at *Les Bons Moments*
each gets his or her own. Foldaway garden numbers
on the terrace, 1950s lab chairs, or simple school pews
under the veranda—forget the traditional Thonets around
the table. Metal chairs are the toast of the town at the moment,
the most famous being unquestionably the Fermob and Tolix
models. Designed primarily for public use, their technical
qualities are abundantly clear: they can be set up and stored
easily—and they last. Foldable or stackable, various models
have long been part of the landscape: the "Model A"
in steel sheet by Tolix, the "Bistro" model with wooden
slats for cafés, or Fermob's "Luxembourg" in tubing
(from the famous Paris garden). And what is the proof of
this success? The models are still in production.

ADDRESS BOOK

Itineraries

The following addresses are among the author's favorite spots for antique hunting and for general wanders around France. Traditionally, flea markets are open Saturday, Sunday, as well as Monday or Friday. The majority of the stores are open from Friday to Sunday. Others may only be open by appointment, so it's always advisable to call up before setting out.

In the following list, the addresses of brocantes featured in the book appear in bold followed by the corresponding page number. For the other places, a brief description indicates the style of merchandise that can be found there. The section is organized by geographic location for ease of use while traveling in France. When calling from outside of France, the country code is +33, and the initial zero is dropped from the phone number.

NORTH PARIS

The Puces at Saint-Ouen constitute one of the most extensive hunting grounds of all (seventeen acres of stands and no less than thirteen markets).

A visit to the Marché Vernaison is well worth it for the cozy charm of its passageways and to the Marché Paul Bert for the exceptional quality of its wares. Finish off with a stroll around Montmartre, then down to the Batignolles quarter, or via the vintage stores just outside Les Abbesses, on avenue Trudaine.

LE GRENIER DE MONET
A mini cabinet of curiosities.
Puces de Saint-Ouen / Marché Vernaison
Aisle 1, stand 28 / 93400 Saint-Ouen
06 07 64 22 65

MOMENTS & MATIÈRES p. 12–19
Puces de Saint-Ouen / Marché Vernaison
Aisle 1, stands 13 and 27 / 93400 Saint-Ouen
06 77 64 87 12

L'OBJET QUI PARLE . . . p. 20–23
86 rue des Martyrs / 75018 Paris
06 09 67 05 30

PAGES 50/70
Retro-design, as its name implies.
15 rue Yvonne le Tac / 75018 Paris
01 42 52 48 59

LA PETITE MAISON
First-class antiques and vintage.
Puces de Saint-Ouen
10 rue Paul Bert / 93400 Saint-Ouen
01 40 10 56 69

SOUS LES TOITS DE PARIS p. 24–29
1 place du docteur Félix Lobligeois / 75017 Paris
01 46 27 75 49

YOMING
Revamped pieces and laid-back creations, "made in Batignolles."
95 rue Nollet / 75017 Paris
01 46 27 76 97 / www.yoming.fr

YONOÏ
Smaller industrial, vintage or ceramic wares.
28 rue Durantin / 75018 Paris
06 10 08 43 66

ZUT!
Quality industrial.
9 rue Ravignan / 75018 Paris
01 42 59 69 68

EAST PARIS
Rue Oberkampf, Marché Popincourt, with a bypass by the Canal Saint-Martin, for a trendier vintage experience.

ALASINGLINGLIN
14 rue Ternaux / 75011 Paris
01 43 38 45 54

ATELIER 154 p. 32–39
154 rue Oberkampf / 75011 Paris
06 62 32 79 06 / www.atelier154.com

BELLE LURETTE p. 40
5 rue du Marché Popincourt
75011 Paris / 01 43 38 67 39

BROKATIK
Industrial and urban-style pieces.
2 rue de l'Hôpital Saint-Louis / 75010 Paris
01 42 40 10 34

LA GARÇONNIÈRE p. 46–49
6 rue du Marché Popincourt / 75011 Paris
06 60 63 32 55 / www.lagarconniere.fr

LOULOU LES AMES ARTS
Smaller vintage ware and lamps for the home.
104 quai de Jemmapes / 75010 Paris
01 42 00 91 39

LA MAISON p. 40–43
3 rue Neuve Popincourt
75011 Paris / 01 48 06 59 47

TROLLS & PUCES p. 40
1 rue du Marché Popincourt
75011 Paris / 01 43 14 60 00

RIGHT BANK, LEFT BANK
Toward the center of Paris and worth making a beeline for when the biennial fair at the Bastille is in town, or during the major springtime clear-out on the rue de Bretagne. Contact the Paris tourist office (0892 68 3000) for exact dates.

LE 106
Natty industrial.
106 rue Vieille du Temple / 75003 Paris
01 42 78 45 71

L'ART DU TEMPS
Workshop furnishings and grunge industrial.
63 rue de Charonne / 75011 Paris
01 47 00 29 30

L'ATTRAPE-COEUR
Classy stock and curios.
24 bis rue Gassendi / 75014 Paris
01 45 38 51 78

AU BON USAGE
From Thonet downwards.
21 rue Saint-Paul / 75004 Paris
01 42 78 80 14

LE COMPTOIR DU CHINEUR
1950s–1980s bazaar.
49 rue Saint-Paul / 75004 Paris
01 42 72 47 39

ET CAETERA
Stylish vintage and pretty curios.
40 rue de Poitou / 75003 Paris
01 42 71 37 11

GALERIE SALON
A Gustavien-style gallery par excellence.
4 rue de Bourbon le château / 75006 Paris
06 62 49 88 81 / www.galeriesalon.com

HÉTÉROCLITE
Fun emporium with smaller vintage wares.
111 rue Vaugirard / 75006 Paris
01 45 48 44 51

L'HEURE BLEUE p. 58–61
17 rue Saint-Roch / 75001 Paris
01 42 60 23 22

MAMIE-GÂTEAUX p. 62–67
70 rue du Cherche-Midi / 75006 Paris
01 45 44 36 63 / www.mamie-gateaux.com

AU PETIT BONHEUR LA CHANCE
Retro kitchenware, stationery.
13 rue Saint-Paul / 75004 Paris
01 42 74 36 38

AUX TROIS SINGES p. 52–57
23 rue Saint-Paul / 75004 Paris
01 42 72 73 69

VIVEMENT JEUDI
Art brocante for people in the know.
La Maison sous le grand arbre
55 rue Mouffetard / 75014 Paris
01 43 31 44 52

WEST PARIS
Chic neighborhoods with some fun addresses. Neuilly, Boulogne, then continuing with an exploration of the Yvelines to Montfort l'Amaury.

AGAPÈ p. 74–81
91 avenue Jean Baptiste Clément
92100 Boulogne-Billancourt
01 47 12 04 88 / www.agapedeco.com

BEAUMARIÉ
Bric-a-brac, wrought iron piles, and doors.
227 rue de Versailles / 92410 Ville-d'Avray
01 47 09 20 37

BOIS L'ÉPICIER
A village famous for its antiques.
Route de Rambouillet / 78550 Maulette
06 81 28 20 55

LES BONHEURS DE SOPHIE
Country-style vintage.
2 route de Marcq / 78770 Andelu
01 34 87 47 42

COLETTE BOUQUET JACOILLOT
Country-style vintage.
4 rue du vieux Village / 78113 Condé-sur-Vesgre
01 34 87 04 64

FILLE D'AVRIL
Bric-a-brac . . . for the girls!
4 rue de Paris / 78490 Montfort l'Amaury
01 34 86 26 09

ORIGINES
Exceptional materials.
Route de Bû / 78550 Houdan
01 30 88 15 15 / www.origines.fr

PEAU D'ANE
Bric-a-brac and interiors.
4 rue de l'Oasis / 92800 Puteaux
01 47 62 97 58

VERT DE GRIS p. 70–73
6 rue Ernest Deloison / 92200 Neuilly-sur-Seine
01 47 38 64 89

NORTHERN FRANCE AND BELGIUM
*Organize your itinerary so as not to bypass
the jumble sales at Lille, at Amiens or Abbeville.*

À LA PAGE
Linens, dishware, and no-stress patinas.
2 rue du Prévot / 1050 Bruxelles / Belgium
+32 (0)2 537 33 04

ALAIN VAN DER GUCHT
One-of-a-kind curiosities.
24 rue Rollebeek / 1000 Bruxelles / Belgium
+32 (0)475 813 646 / www.curiosities.be

APOSTROPHE
Great industrial design.
50 rue Blaes / 1000 Bruxelles / Belgium
+32 (0)2 502 67 38 / www.apostrophe1.com

BORDS D'EAUX p. 88–91
35 rue Jules Barni / 80350 Mers-les-Bains
02 35 50 12 65

LA BROCANTE À LA FERME
Piles of bric-a-brac.
18 route de Bapaume / 59400 Cambrai
03 27 70 31 50

LA BROCANTE DE LA BRUYÈRE
p. 84–87
32 rue Campion / 60880 Le Meux
03 44 91 12 77

BROKIDÉE
64 rue Pasteur / 59700 Marcq-en-Baroeul
03 20 13 82 02 / www.brokidee.fr

CHEZ PATRICK DELOISON
Charming seaside vintage.
1 quai Romerel / 80230 Saint-Valéry-sur-Somme
03 22 26 92 17

ESPACE NORD-OUEST p. 92–96
644 avenue du Général de Gaulle
59910 Bondues / 03 20 03 38 39
www.nordouestantiquites.com

LE GRENIER DU CHT'I
Not unlike Espace Nord-Ouest.
37 rue Charles Gounod / 59100 Roubaix
03 20 24 94 94

LE JARDIN PERDU
Country vintage . . . in an urban setting.
101 rue Haute / 1050 Bruxelles / Belgium
+32 (0)497 295 307

LE MARCHAND D'OUBLIS p. 92
70 rue Jean-Bapiste Lebas / 59910 Bondues
03 20 11 25 79

LE PETIT PAGE
Tons of toys.
72 rue Page / 1050 Bruxelles / Belgium
+32 (0)2 534 64 00

LA RESSOURCERIE
Vintage and local creations.
Wazemmes / 43 rue du Marché / 59000 Lille
03 20 48 09 28

TOUS LES JOURS DIMANCHE . . . p. 92
13 rue Masurel / 59000 Lille
03 28 36 05 92

WADDINGTONS
CLUEDO
ective
PENALTY!
A Pepys CARD GAME
NEW IMPROVED EDITION
THE WORLD FAMOUS FOOTBALL GAME
SPORTS

NORMANDY

Wait for the weekend and then head for the seaside, through the towns and villages of Normandy that are dotted with amazing vintage stores.

LA BROCANTE DU MONT MIREL
Stacks of quality industrial furniture.
15 route de Pont-Audemer / 27260 Cormeilles
02 32 42 91 48

L'ÉMOI D'ÉTÉ
Elegant vintage.
19 rue de Paris / 14360 Trouville-sur-Mer
02 31 88 94 64

FANETTE W. p. 100–103
93 rue d'Amiens / 76000 Rouen
02 35 73 49 77

GARBO
Vintage deco and art.
21 place du Général de Gaulle / 27260 Cormeilles
06 10 67 31 51

JACOTTE & JAVOTTE
Fun English-style vintage.
34 rue Saint-Nicolas / 76000 Rouen
02 35 15 93 29

MISE EN SCÈNE p. 100
76 rue des Bains / 14360 Trouville-sur-Mer
02 31 81 91 55

ORIOT ANTIQUITÉS
Fine vintage and art.
14 rue des Capucins / 14600 Honfleur
02 31 89 70 04

LA ROSE DES VENTS
Fifties and designer vintage and chic secondhand clothing too.
37 rue Saint-Nicolas / 76000 Rouen
02 35 70 29 78

LA SERRE p. 106–111
Route de Cormeilles / 14130 Bonneville-la-Louvet
02 31 64 03 21

LA VIE À LA CAMPAGNE
An expert in vintage garden ware.
39 rue Haute / 14600 Honfleur
02 31 88 47 83

LA PERCHE

In the south of Normandy, in the département of L'Orne, Le Perche region offers both pastoral beauty and unsurpassed vintage shopping itineraries.

CYRILLE FASSIER
Family style.
7 rue Pont Boivin / 61110 Longny-au-Perche
02 33 73 56 21

GABRIELLE FEUILLARD p. 126–127
10 rue Ville-close / 61130 Bellême
02 33 73 53 82

L'INDISCRET
Vintage as we love it.
La Percheronnette / 8 rue Basse
28330 Authon-du-Perche / 02 37 49 13 69

LA MAISON D'HORBÉ p. 122–125
Le Bourg / 61360 La Perrière
02 33 73 18 41

LA MAISON FASSIER p. 114–121
55 rue de l'Eglise / 61110 Rémalard
02 33 73 56 21

PATRICK LAMIROTÉ
Ironwork and general bric-a-brac.
5 rue des Vanneries / 61110 Mortagne-au-Perche
02 33 25 35 91

VILLAGE DU VAL D'HUISNE p. 128–133
A whole village of brocanteurs.
RN23 direction Nogent-le-Rotrou
28400 Nogent-le-Rotrou
06 86 93 10 15

WESTERN FRANCE

From the Loire River to the sea, from the castles of Anjou to the pink granite coast, here culture, countryside, and brocantes flourish together. Don't forget the Sunday gatherings around the Loire (Montsoreau, Chinon, Montreuil-sur-Bellay, and so on) and the summer fairs at Saint-Méloire-des-Ondes, Lanvollon, and Ploemeur-Bodou.

ANGES ET DÉMONS p. 136–141
14 rue Notre Dame / 49350 Cunault
06 03 56 09 26

AU BOUT DU MONDE p. 142–143
Quai des Terre-Neuvas / 22370 Pléneuf-Val-André
02 96 63 18 84

LA BOUTIQUE BLEUE
A charming spot.
55 place de la Fontaine / 37500 Chinon
06 07 33 69 81

LA BROCANTE DE LA MARINE DE LOIRE
Smaller wares and interiors in a splendid house.
9 quai de la Loire / 49730 Montsoreau
02 41 50 18 21

LA "CHINE" DE NICOLAS
Chic seaside vintage.
6 boulevard de la Houle / 35800 Saint-Briac-sur-Mer
02 99 88 06 96

COMPTOIRS DE L'OUEST
Large hall with bric-a-brac and decoration.
Quai des Terre-Neuvas / 22370 Pléneuf-Val-André
02 96 63 05 85

LE FOU DE BASSAN
Vintage from around the world.
Port de Locquémeau / 22300 Locquémeau
02 96 35 22 27

LA LANGOUSTE BLEUE
Seaside knickknacks.
44 Grande Rue / 35800 Saint-Briac-sur-Mer
02 99 88 36 98

LA MAISON BLEUE p. 144–149
Moulin de la Ville Geffroy / 22170 Plélo
02 96 74 13 63

MAISON BROCANTE
A charming spot.
15 rue Ernest Renan / 22220 Tréguier
02 96 92 42 70

LA SEIGNEURIE
Manor house with stock of excellent taste.
35114 Saint-Benoît-des-Ondes
02 99 58 62 96

YANNICK LAFOURCADE
Trade and craft wares and linens.
22 Haute-Rue / 49730 Montsoreau
02 41 50 72 12

SOUTHWEST FRANCE

What with the four colors of the Périgord, the pleasures of Bordeaux, the traditional Quinconces *fair, and then a run around the Bassin d'Arcachon or onto the bustling Île de Ré, there's more than enough here to keep you busy.*

LE 100 M2
Loft style and homemade bags.
84 cours Lamarque de Plaisance / 33120 Arcachon
05 56 83 10 14

LE 20
Festive wine bar and vintage.
9 route de Saint-Clément / 17590 Ars-en-Ré
05 46 29 69 52

ANNE GROS
Vintage finery and piles of fine linen.
Le Canon 165 route Cap Ferret / 33950 Lège-Cap-Ferret
05 56 03 60 00

LES ANTIQUITÉS DE FABRICE PEZON
An individual style.
22 rue Jean Macé / 24100 Bergerac
06 85 21 13 63

ANTIQUITÉS LA MALINE
Engaging vintage stock.
42 rue du Gors Jonc / 17880 Les Portes-en-Ré
05 46 29 56 77

ANTIQUITÉS RUGGERI (1900–1970)
1900–1970 in a nutshell.
107 rue Notre-Dame / 33000 Bordeaux
06 09 72 21 98

LES BAINS DE MER
Full of surprises.
La Croix-Michaud / 17630 La Flotte-en-Ré
06 81 79 35 93

LE BIGORNEAU LANGOUREUX
Seaside vintage and pictures.
16 rue Charles Biret / 17630 La Flotte-en-Ré
05 46 09 95 58

LE CAFÉ-BROCANTE DU COUVENT
An eatery with tapas and vintage.
23 rue du Couvent / 33000 Bordeaux
05 56 44 15 20

LES CAMPANI
Quintessentially Île de Ré.
30 rue Aristide Briand / 17410 Saint-Martin-de-Ré
05 46 09 27 70

CÔTÉ JARDIN
A brocante with its finger on the pulse.
Place du Marché / 17590 Ars-en-Ré
05 46 29 29 61

L'ESPRIT DU CAP p. 160–163
2 rue des Pionniers / 33950 Lège-Cap-Ferret
05 56 60 67 79

GALERIE KAHN
Industrial design and art gallery.
Place du Marché / 17590 Ars-en-Ré
06 09 10 63 89

LA MAISON DU BASSIN
Fine antiques and novelties.
Promenade du Bassin / 24150 Lalinde
05 53 61 20 19

MARCHÉ EIFFEL
Fine building materials from town and country.
17 rue Notre-Dame / 33000 Bordeaux
05 56 51 61 63

PASSAGE SAINT-MICHEL p. 152–159
14, 17 place Canteloup / 33800 Bordeaux
05 56 92 14 76 / www.passage-st-michel.com

SWANN
Pretty seaside vintage.
17 boulevard de la côte d'Argent / 33120 Arcachon
05 56 83 29 55

LA TREILLE MARINE p. 164–169
4 place de la République / 17410 Saint-Martin-de-Ré
05 46 09 36 22

PROVENCE

It's always worth taking the legendary highway, the "Nationale 7." Burgundy, Lyon, L'Isle-sur-la-Sorgue, with a stop-off at the Barjac *fair, a detour via the* Route des Antiquaires *at Pézenas, then ending with a dip into the markets at Nice or Antibes.*

AUX 4 SOUS
A huge and well-known bric-a-brac.
1719 Route de Privas / 7400 Meysse
04 75 52 92 88 / www.brocante-4sous.com

Acknowledgments

To all the *brocanteurs*, people ruled by passion more than reason, who opened the doors to their exquisite and often intimate stores while this book was being written. To Ghislaine Bavoillot, Aurélie Sallandrouze, Sylvie Ramaut, Kate Mascaro, Tessa Anglin, and to the whole team at Flammarion and their taste for good living. At Farrow and Ball, to Vanessa Fratti and Beverly Collins in particular for the visuals for the Ringwold Papers collection of wallpaper that kicks off each chapter. USA / Farrow & Ball Showrooms / New York, Greenwich, Boston, Los Angeles, Washington, and Chicago / +1 (888) 511 1121 / www.farrow-ball.com To Guy Lucas and Olympus France, www.olympus.fr

At the tourist offices, regional and local tourist councils, especially to Sylvie Blin, Cécile Broc, Sabine Canonica, Nathalie Coupau, Alain Étienne, Marie-Yvonne Holley, Christine Kervadec, Armelle Le Goff, Micheline Morissonneau, Raphaëlle Nicaise, Patricia de Pouzilhac, Hélène Ramsamy, Carole Rauber, Blandine Thenet, and Gwenaëlle Towse.

Comité Régional de Tourisme, Aquitaine
www.tourisme-aquitaine.fr
Comité Départemental de Tourisme, Dordogne
www.dordogne-perigord.com
Comité Départemental de Tourisme, Gironde
www.tourisme-gironde.com
Bordeaux Tourism Office
www.bordeaux-tourisme.com
Comité Départemental de Tourisme, Anjou
www.anjou-tourisme.com
Comité Départemental de Tourisme, Calvados
www.calvados-tourisme.com
Comité Régional de Tourisme, Languedoc-Roussillon
www.sunfrance.com
Comité Régional de Tourisme, Nord-Pas-de-Calais
www.crt-nordpasdecalais.fr
Comité Départemental de Tourisme, l'Orne
www.ornetourisme.com
Comité Régional de Tourisme, Provence-Alpes-Côte d'Azur
www.decouverte-paca.fr
Comité Régional de Tourisme, Rhône-Alpes
www.rhonealpes-tourisme.com
and www.rhonesalpes.tv
Lyon Tourism Office
www.onlylyon.org
Comité Départemental de Tourisme, Ardêche
www.ardeche-guide.com

And to all the regular and occasional readers of *Bord de mer* and other delights . . . for their complicity.

Translated from the French by David Radzinowicz
Copyediting: Emily Ligniti
Design: Sébastien Siraudeau
Typesetting: Thomas Gravemaker
Proofreading: Helen Adedotun
Color Separation: Penez, Lille, France
All photographs were taken with the e-system

Distributed in North America by Rizzoli International Publications, Inc.

Simultaneously published in French as *Brocantes*
© Flammarion, Paris, 2008

English-language edition
© Flammarion, 2008

Dépôt légal: 10/2008

Printed in Singapore by Tien Wah Press
07 08 09 3 2 1

ISBN: 978-2-0803-0054-6